THE ST. AUGUSTINE LIFEGUIDE

Also from St. Augustine's Press

The John Paul II LifeGuide

The St. Augustine LifeGuide

Words to Live by from the Great Christian Saint

St. Augustine

Translated by Silvano Borruso

A LifeGuide™ Series Title

ST. AUGUSTINE'S PRESS
South Bend, Indiana
2006

Manufactured in the United States of America.

1 2 3 4 5 6   11 10 09 08 07 06

Library of Congress Cataloging in Publication Data
Augustine, Saint, Bishop of Hippo.
[Selections. English & Latin. 2005]
The St. Augustine LifeGuide: words to live by
from the great Christian saint / St. Augustine;
translated by Silvano Borruso.
p. cm. – (A LifeGuide series title)
English and Latin.
Includes index.
ISBN 1-58731-756-7 (pbk.: alk. paper)
1. Theology – Miscellanea. 2. Christian life –
Miscellanea. I. Title: Saint Augustine LifeGuide.
II. Borruso, Silvano. III. Title. IV. Series.
BR65.A52E6 2005
230'.14–dc22   2005029092

∞ The paper used in this publication meets the minimum
requirements of the American National Standard for
Information Sciences – Permanence of Paper for Printed
Materials, ANSI Z39.48-1984.

St. Augustine's Press
www.staugustine.net

Contents

TRANSLATOR'S INTRODUCTION

This book lists 200 quotes from the works of St Augustine of Hippo, from his earliest *De Ordine* written at Cassiciacum near Milan in 386 to the unfinished work against Julian (428–429) shortly before Augustine's death in 430.

The quotes are cited as follows:

AAC: Against the Academicians (*Contra Academicos*). Milan 386.

AAD: Against Adimantum (*Contra Adimantum Manichaei discipulum*). Hippo 394.

ACS: Against Cresconium (*Ad Cresconium Grammaticum Partis Donati*). Hippo 406.

AGF: Against Faustus (*Contra Faustum Manichaeum*). Hippo 400.

AJL: Unfinished work against Julian's second answer *(Opus imperfectum contra secundam Iuliani Responsionem)*. Hippo 428–429.

BPT: On the Uniqueness of Baptism *(De Unico Baptismo)*. Hippo 410.

CAT: Rudiments of Catechism *(De Catechizandis Rudibus)*. Hippo 400.

CCC: Customs of the Catholic Church *(De Moribus Ecclesiae Catholicae)*. Rome 389.

CFS: The Confessions *(Confessionum Libri XIII)*. Hippo 397–401.

CNT: On Continence *(De Continentia)*. Year and place uncertain.

COG: The City of God *(De Civitate Dei)*. Hippo 423–426.

DOR: De Ordine *(De Ordine)*. Cassiciacum 386.

LET: Letters *(Epistolae)*. Various places 391–430.

NAG: Nature and Grace (*De Natura et Gratia*). Hippo 415.

OAE: On the Agreement of the Evangelists (*De Consensu Evangelistarum*). Hippo 400–402.

OCD: On Christian Doctrine (*De Doctrina Christiana*). Hippo 397–426.

OFW: On Free Will (*De Libero Arbitrio et Gratia*). Hippo 426–427.

OHV: On Holy Virginity (*De Sancta Virginitate*). Hippo 401.

ONM: On Music (*De Musica*). Cassiciacum, Rome 387–389.

OPS: Commentaries on the Psalms (*Enarrationes in Psalmos*). Years 391–430.

OTR: On the True Religion (*De Vera Religione*). Tagaste 389.

OTS: On the Soul and its Origin (*De Anima et Eius Origine*). Hippo 423–424.

SRM: Sermons (*Sermones*). Various places 391–430.

OWD: On widowhood (*De Bono Viduitatis*). Hippo 414.

TJEp: Treatise on St John's Letter (*In Ioannis Epistolam Tractatus*). Hippo 416.

TJEv: Treatise on St John's Gospel (*In Ioannis Evangelium Tractatus*). Hippo 416.

The Translation

The Latin text is offered side by side with the English translation for two reasons:

1. No translation, however accurate, can possibly render Augustine's inimitable classical Latin style;

2. Suggestions from readers toward a better rendering than the one offered here are most welcome.

The translation is original, and no other translation has been consulted. Should any rendering be similar or even identical to any of existing translations, it is a matter of pure coincidence.

Thanks are due to Martyn Drakard for his most useful suggestions toward polishing the text and to Fr. Franco Monteverde for supplying texts hard to find.

Silvano Borruso
28th August 2005
Feast of St. Augustine

ORDER

1. *Causa constitutae universitatis, et lux perci-piendae veritatis et fons bibendae felicitatis.*
    COG 8, 10, 2.

    [God is] the cause of the order of the universe, the light to perceive its truths and the spring to drink happiness from.

2. *Pax omnium rerum tranquillitas ordinis.*
    COG 19, 13.

    The peace of all things is the tranquillity of order.

3. *Minus ordinata inquieta sunt. Ordinantur et quiescunt.* CFS 13, 9.

    Lack of order produces restlessness. Where there is order there is peace.

4. *Ordo est quem si tenuerimus in vita perducet ad Deum, et quem nisi tenuerimus in vita, non perveniemus ad Deum.* DOR 1, IX, 27.

    Order is what leads us to God, provided

we live it. If we fail to live it, we shall not
attain God.

5.   *Si quis temere ac sine ordine disciplinarum in
harum rerum cognitionem audet irruere, pro
docto credulum, pro cauto incredulum fit.*
DOR 2, IV, 17.

Anyone who rushes into learning such
disciplines rashly and without order,
becomes not a scholar but a seeker after
vain curiosity, gullible instead of learned,
unbelieving instead of prudent.

6.   *Adolescentibus ergo studiosis eius ita viven-
dum est ut a venereis rebus, ab illecebris ven-
tris et gutturis, ab immodesto corporis cultu et
ornatu, ab inanibus negotiis ludorum, a tor-
pore somni atque pigritiae, ab aemulatione,
obtrectatione, invidentia, ab honorum pote-
statumque ambitionibus, ab ipsius etiam
laudis immodica cupiditate se abstineant.*
DOR 2, VIII, 25.

You, youthful students, must begin by
abstaining from sex, from the enticement
of gluttony and drunkenness, an immod-
est concern for body and dress, pointless
sports and games, the heaviness of too

much sleep and laziness, vain competition, detraction, envy, ambition for status and power, and even from the excessive desire for simple praise.

7. *Non est diu quod habet extremum.* OPS 30, II. d. 1, 8.

What has an end does not last.

GOD:
FATHER, SON, AND HOLY SPIRIT

8. *Ipse finis erit desideriorum nostrorum, qui sine fine videbitur, sine fastidio amabitur, sine fatigatione laudabitur.* COG 22, 30.

God is the object of our desires, to be contemplated unceasingly, loved with no trace of boredom, and tirelessly praised.

9. *Nosti quid facias de agro tuo, et nescit Deus quid faciat de servo suo?* OPS 63, 19.

You know what to do with your farm, and does God not know what to do with you, his servant?

10. *Intendat caritas vestra: Deus ineffabilis est; facilius dicimus quid non sit, quam quid sit.* OPS 85, 12.

May your love understand this: God is ineffable. We find it much easier to say what He is not than to say what He is.

11. *Amor qui semper ardes et numquam extingueris, caritas, Deus meus, accende me!* CFS 10, 29.

O love, you who always burn without being quenched, charity, my God, set me on fire!

12. *Ille placet Deo cui placet Deus.* OPS 32, II, 1, d. 1.

He pleases God who is pleased with God.

13. *Est somnus animae, est somnus corporis. Somnus animae est oblivisci Deum suum.* OPS 62, 3.

There is a sleep of the soul and a sleep of the body. The sleep of the soul is to be unmindful of God.

14. *Deus impossibilia non iubet, sed iubendo monet et facere quod possis, et petere quod non possis.* NAG 43, 50.

God does not command impossible things. He prompts you to do what you can, and to ask Him for what you cannot.

15. *[Auctoritas divina] non teneri sensibus, quibus videntur illa miranda, sed ad intellectum iubet evolare, simul demonstrans et*

quanta hic possit et cur haec faciat et quam parvi pendat. DOR 2, IX, 27.

[Divine authority] commands us not to remain at the level of the senses, which are taken in by anything attractive, but to soar to the level of the intellect, showing what marvels we can achieve, why, and how little we value them.

16. *Cantate vocibus, cantate cordibus, cantate oribus, cantate moribus. Cantate Domino canticum novum.* SRM 34, 6.

Sing with your voices, sing with your hearts, with your lips and with your conduct. Sing a new song to the Lord.

17. *Novus homo, novum Testamentum, novum canticum . . . cantet canticum novum non lingua, sed vita.* OPS 32, II, d. 1, 8.

A new man, a new covenant, a new song . . . let him sing the new song not with the lips but with life.

18. *Hoc est enim bene canere Deo, in iubilatione cantare.* OPS 32, II, d. 1, 8.

There is one way to sing to God: sing with joy.

19. *Tu autem eras interior intimo meo et superior summo meo.* CFS 3, 6.

You were deep inside me, and way above my highest inner self.

20. *Tu bone omnipotens, qui sic curas unumquemque nostrum tamquam solus cures, et sic omnes tamquam singulos.* CFS 3, 11.

How good you are, almighty God, caring for each one of us as if you had nothing else to do and as if we were all one and the same.

21. *Noli aliquid dicere sine illo, et non dicit aliquid sine te.* OPS 85, 1.

Don't say anything godless, and He will not say anything without taking you into account.

22. *Secretum Dei intentos debet facere, non adversos.* TJEv 27, 2.

The mystery of God ought to make us intent on good, not stubborn.

23. *Unum Deum omnipotentem eumque tripotentem, Patrem et Filium et Spiritum Sanctum docent veneranda mysteria, quae fide* *sincera et inconcussa populos liberant.* DOR 2, IV, 16.

The venerable mysteries teach the one God almighty and thrice powerful, Father, Son and Holy Spirit. Such sincere and unshaken faith sets free entire nations.

24. *Sagittaveras tu cor nostrum caritate tua, et gestabamus verba tua transfixa visceribus.* CFS 9, 2.

You had pierced our hearts with the shaft of your love. We were carrying about your words thrust deep into our inner-most being.

25. *Verbi enim Dei inanis est forinsecus praedicator qui non est intus auditor.* SRM 179, 1.

It is a waste of time to preach the word of God without first listening to it within oneself.

26. *Interior ergo magister est qui docet. Christus docet, inspiratio ipsius docet.* TJEp 3, 13.

The teacher who instructs is within. Christ is the teacher, his very inspiration teaches.

27. *Extende caritatem per totum orbem, si vis Christum amare; quia membra Christi per orbem iacent.* TJEp 7, 2.

Extend your charity everywhere if you want to love Christ, for the members of Christ are to be found everywhere.

28. *Deseruerunt illi sponsorem salutis, honoravit ille socium crucis.* OTS 1, 9.

They deserted Him who promised salvation; He honored one crucified together with Him.

29. *Timeo enim Iesum transeuntem.* SRM 88, 14.

I fear Jesus passing by.

30. *Domine, si sine te nihil, totum in te.* OPS 30, II, d. 1, 4.

Lord, if there is nothing apart from You, then everything is in You.

31. *Christe, responde, vince atque convince. Clama: Sine me nihil potestis facere, ut taceant qui clamant: Etsi difficilius, tamen possemus et sine te facere.* AJL 2, 198.

Christ, answer us and conquer our hearts. Shout: "Without me you can do nothing."

Silence those who claim: "However diffi-
cult it may be, we can do without you."

32. *Nam sine illo, nos nihil; in illo autem, ipse
Christus et nos.* OPS 30, 1.

Without Christ we are nothing. With
Him, Christ and we are one.

33. *Iesus neminem timuit in humilitate. Timebit
quemquam in claritate?* OPS 93, 7.

Jesus feared no one in His earthly humility. Will he fear anyone in his everlasting
splendor?

34. *Amicitia non est vera, nisi cum ea tu agglu-
tinas inter inhaerentes tibi caritate diffusa in
cordibus nostris per Spiritum Sanctum qui
datus est nobis.* CFS 4, 4.

There is no true friendship if the glue
that makes it stick is not the love of God
poured into our hearts by the Holy Spirit
that has been given to us.

HUMAN LIFE

35. *Uno verbo a bestiis, quod rationale; et alio a divinis separatur, quod mortale dicitur.* DOR 2, XI, 31.

The term "rational" sets us apart from the beasts, and the term "mortal" from God.

36. *Quando autem melior et pecoribus praeponendo? Quando novit quod facit. At nihil aliud me pecori praeponit, nisi quod rationale animal sum.* DOR 2, XIX, 49.

When should one be deemed superior to cattle? When one knows what one does. Nothing but reason makes me higher than the beasts.

37. *Non numerosa faciendo, sed numeros cognoscendo melior sum.* DOR 2, XIX, 49.

I am superior not for doing a large number of things, but for knowing what number is.

38.   *Duos pedes habeto, noli esse claudus.* OPS 33,
          d. 2, 10.

          Stand on your two feet; don't waver.

39.   *Melius enim utique tota die foderent quam
          tota die saltarent.* OPS 32, II, d. 1, 6.

          It is far better to spend the whole day
          hoeing than dancing.

40.   *Delectatio quippe quasi pondus est animae.*
          ONM 6, 11.

          Pleasure acts indeed as a dead weight for
          the soul.

41.   *Mens nostra pruriens in auribus.* CFS 4, 8.

          Our mind was corrupted by itching ears.

42.   *Aliud est enim quod in agendo anteponitur,
          aliud quod pluris in appetendo aestimatur.*
          DOR 2, IX, 26.

          What gets done first is one thing; what one
          really intends to do is entirely another.

43.   *Quis autem veraciter laudat, nisi qui sinceri-
          ter amat?* LET 140, 18.

Who honestly gives praise, except the one who really loves?

44. *Quid prodest strepitus oris muto corde?* TJEv 9, 13.

Of what use is to shout at a dumb heart?

45. *Fluitat humana memoria per varias cogitationes, nec in cuiusquam potestate est quid et quando ei veniat in mentem.* OAE 3, 13.

Human memory flutters from one thought to another, and it is not in anyone's power to determine what may come to mind and when.

46. *Omnis qui sibi vult aliquid praestari, in ardore est desiderii: ipsum desiderium sitis est animae.* OPS 62, 5.

Whoever wants something badly, burns with desire: that very desire is the thirst of the soul.

47. *In quibuslibet rebus humanis nihil est homini amicum sine homine amico.* LET 130, 4.

Nothing is friendly in any human situation if there is no friend around.

48.   *Inimicitias vitent cautissime, ferant aequis-*
sime, finiant citissime. DOR 2, VIII, 25.

Avoid enmity most carefully, bear it as
calmly as you can, and bring it to an end
as quickly as possible.

49.   *Attendite non praesumere de pecunia, de*
amico homine, de honore et iactantia saeculi.
OPS 131, 25.

Beware of taking for granted money,
friends, worldly honors and vanities.

50.   *Amorem autem pecuniae totius suae spei cer-*
tissimum venenum esse credant. DOR 2, VIII,
25.

Know that the love of money is the certain dashing of all your hopes.

51.   *Ubi enim mihi animus erga me hominis*
ignotus est et incertus, melius arbitror melio-
ra sentire quam inexplorata culpare. OTS
1, 2.

If I am ignorant and uncertain of some-
one's true sentiments toward me, I prefer
to think well rather than condemn what I
don't know.

52. *Nunc autem nescio. Nec me pudet, ut istum, fateri nescire quod nescio.* OTS 1, 15.

I simply don't know. I am not ashamed, as he is, to admit that I don't know what I don't know.

53. *Versa et reversa, in tergum et in latera et ventrem et dura sunt omnia: et tu solus requies.* CFS 6, 16.

The soul turns over and over, lying on its back, belly, or side, and finds all of them hard. Only You offer true rest.

54. *Quamobrem otium sanctum quaerit caritas veritatis, negotium iustum suscipit necessitas caritatis.* COG 19, 19.

The love of truth seeks holiness in leisure, and the need of love seeks justice in business.

55. *Nimis inimica amicitia, seductio mentis investigabilis . . . cum dicitur: Eamus, faciamus, et pudet non esse impudentem.* CFS 2, 9.

What a truly dangerous friendship! How can the mind be so sidetracked and deceived into being greedy . . . by the "let

us just do it" mentality. And one becomes
ashamed of not being shameless.

56.   *Sicut amici adulantes pervertunt, sic inimici
litigantes plerumque corrigunt.* CFS 9, 8.

As flattering friends pervert, so quarreling
enemies more often than not correct.

57.   *Suspectus est nescio quis quasi inimicus, et
forte est amicus. Videtur alter quasi amicus,
et est forsitan occultus inimicus. O tenebrae!*
SRM 49, 4.

A reputed enemy turns out to be a friend.
Another one, who looks friendly, is per-
haps a secret enemy. How hard it is to
tell!

58.   *Hoc enim cogitis, ut de bono et de malo, non
scriptoribus et librariis, sed coquis et dulciari-
is ministris vobiscum potius disseramus.* CCC
2, 16.

Mind you: in this argument with you
about good and evil, I will not ask the
views of writers and literati, but of pastry
cooks and bakers.

59. *Nam et feminae sunt apud veteres philosophatae, et philosophia tua mihi plurimum placet.* DOR 1, XI, 31.

There have been plenty of women philosophers in ancient times, and I rather like your philosophy. [To his mother Monica at Cassiciacum.]

60. *Inter ipsas leges carnifex locum necessarium tenet, et in bene moderatae civitatis ordinem inseritur.* DOR 2, IV, 12.

The public executioner holds a necessary office in law, which is part and parcel of the social order of a well-governed State.

61. *Tanta est pernicies animorum, qui cum vincere hominem volunt, ab errore vincuntur.* AAD 28, 2.

So great is the evil of some, that just as they want to dominate others, error dominates them.

62. *Tota vita christiani boni sanctum desiderium est.* TJEp 4, 6.

A good Christian's whole life is a holy desire.

63.   *Magis sunt vivorum solatia quam subsidia mortuorum.* COG 1, 12.

[Funerals] are more a solace for the living than a help for the dead.

64.   *Ama pacem, habe pacem, posside pacem, cape ad te quantos potes ad possidendam pacem: tanto latior erit quanto a pluribus possidebitur.* SRM 357, 1.

Love peace, be at peace, possess peace, and gather around you all those who want to possess it. Peace will spread in proportion to the number of people possessing it.

65.   *O si viderent internum aeternum, quod ego quia gustaveram, frendebam.* CFS 9, 4.

Oh if they could see the eternity of the interior life. I, who had tasted it, fretted at being unable to show it to them.

66.   *Vis audire consilium? Si vis ab illo fugere, ad ipsum fuge.* TJEp 6, 3.

Do you want a piece of advice? If you want to run away from Him, run toward Him.

67. *Quando autem et teipso interior est, non est quo fugias a Deo irato nisi ad Deum placatum: prorsus non est quo fugias.* OPS 74, 9.

Since God is inside you more than you are yourself, you cannot run away from an angry God except to an appeased God. There is nowhere else to run to.

68. *Non stat ergo aetas nostra: ubique fatigatio est, ubique lassitudo, ubique corruptio.* OPS 62, 6.

Our age does not stand still. It's all weariness, tiredness, and corruption.

69. *In isto deserto, quam multipliciter laborat, tam multipliciter sitit; quam multipliciter fatigatur, tam multipliciter sitit illam infatigabilem incorruptionem.* OPS 62, 6.

In this desert, the more one works, the more one thirsts; for one can get tired in many different ways, thus longing in many different ways for that incorruptibility that knows no tiredness.

70. *Finis autem vitae tam longam quam brevem vitam hoc idem facit.* COG 1, 11.

Death makes a long life last the same time as a short one.

TRUTH AND WISDOM

71. *Diligens inquisitor inveniet.* OAE 3, 13, 49.

The careful seeker will always find.

72. *O rerum naturae obscuritas quantum tegmen est falsitatis.* CCC 2, 16, 38.

An unclear understanding of nature becomes a cover for much falsehood.

73. *Mihi istam mentem Deus dedit, ut inveniendae veritati nihil omnino praeponam, nihil aliud velim, nihil cogitem, nihil amem.* DOR 2, XX, 52.

God gave me the resolve not to prefer anything to the search for truth, not to desire, think, or love anything else.

74. *Nam quisquis omnem philosophiam fugiendam putat, nihil nos vult aliud quam non amare sapientiam.* DOR 1, XI, 33.

Whoever condemns philosophy as a whole condemns nothing less than wisdom itself.

75. *Si quisquis volet vitare stultitiam, non eam conetur intellegere.* DOR 2, III, 10.

Anyone who wants to avoid foolishness should not try to understand it.

76. *Cum in rebus ipsis fallacibus ratione totum agere homines moliantur, quid sit ipsa ratio et qualis sit, nisi perpauci prorsus ignorant.* DOR 2, XI, 30.

Most people try to use reason even in deception and falsehood, and so with few exceptions they have no idea of the nature of reason itself or of its qualities.

77. *Eruditio disciplinarum liberalium, modesta sane ac succincta, et alacriores et perseverantiores et comptiores exhibet amatores amplectendae veritatis.* DOR, VIII, 24.

Instruction in the liberal arts, done in moderation and to the point, produces lively, persevering, and refined lovers of truth.

78. *Satis est nihil fieri, nihil gigni quod non aliena causa genuerit ac moverit.* DOR 1, V, 14.

It is enough to know that nothing happens without a cause, and nothing comes into being without being generated.

79. *Promiseram autem, si meministi, me tibi demonstraturum esse aliquid quod sit nostra mente atque ratione sublimius. Ecce tibi, est ipsa veritas: amplectere illam si potes et fruere illa.* OFW 2, 13.

You may remember I promised to show you something higher than our mind and reason. Here it is: truth itself. Embrace the truth if you can, and taste her delights.

80. *Aliud est discere, aliud videri sibi didicisse.* OTS 2, 6.

It is one thing to learn, and entirely another to appear learned.

81. *Cuius erroris maxima causa est, quod homo sibi ipse est incognitus.* DOR 1, I, 3.

The main cause of this error is the lack of self-knowledge.

82. *Molestum et periculosum est cum eo unum fieri quod separari potest.* DOR 2, XVIII, 48.

To force unity on what can be told apart is to invite trouble and danger.

83. *Qui novit veritatem novit eam; qui novit eam, novit aeternitatem. Caritas novit eam. O aeterna veritas, et vera caritas et cara aeternitas! Tu es Deus meus; tibi suspiro die ac nocte.* CFS 7, 10.

Whoever knows the truth, knows the light it brings, and whoever experiences that light knows what eternity is. Love knows it well. O eternal truth, true love and beloved eternity! You are my God, to whom I sigh night and day.

84. *Vates veritatis sunt quicumque possunt esse sapientes.* DOR 1, IV, 10.

Anyone who can attain wisdom is a teacher of truth.

85. *Faciliusque dubitarem vivere me, quam non esse veritatem, quae per ea quae facta sunt intellecta conspicitur.* CFS 7, 10.

I would rather doubt my being alive than that there was no truth, a truth that can be understood and perceived in what He has made.

86. *Quid est enim philosophia? Amor sapientiae.* AAC 2, 3.

And what is philosophy? The love of wisdom.

87. *Ipsum verum non videbis nisi in philosophiam totus intraveris.* AAC 2, 3.

You will not see the truth unless you plunge your whole self into philosophy.

88. *Hoc esse philosophari, amare Deum cuius natura sit incorporalis.* COG 8, 8.

To philosophize is to love God, whose nature is incorporeal.

89. *Nulla est homini causa philosophandi, nisi ut beatus sit.* COG 9, 1.

The only reason to philosophize is to want to be happy.

90. *Se illa ratio ad ipsarum rerum divinarum*

beatissimam contemplationem rapere voluit.
DOR 2, XVI, 44.

Reason wants to soar to the heights of the
contemplation of divine realities.

91. *Dialectice scit scire; sola scientes facere non
solum vult, sed etiam potest.* DOR 2, XIII, 38.

Logic knows that it knows. It alone wants
to make people learned, and has the abil-
ity to do so.

92. *Non enim vere poetica tantum me avertere a
philosophia potest quantum inveniendi veri
diffidentia.* DOR 1, IV, 10.

Poetry cannot lead me away from philosophy. Despair of finding the truth can.

93. *Noli foras ire, in teipsum redi, in interiore
homine habitat veritas. Et si tuam naturam
mutabilem inveneris, transcende et teipsum.
Illuc ergo tende, unde ipsum lume rationis
accenditur.* OTR 39, 72.

Do not venture out. Go into yourself:
truth dwells inside man. And if you find
your nature wavering, go beyond yourself. Aim at where the very light of reason
shines.

94.   *Sapiens eris si te non esse credideris.* OTS 3, 1.

You will be wise only when you don't believe you are.

95.   *Haec praecipue cave, fili, si vis esse victor erroris, nec te, quando aliquid nescis, existimes scire, sed ut scias, disce nescire.* OTS 4, 24.

Pay heed to this advice when you want to conquer error: when you don't know something, do not presume to know. And when you want to know, first acknowledge that you don't know.

96.   *Impia mens odit etiam ipsum intellectum.* SRM 156, 1.

An evil mind hates understanding.

97.   *Homo aliquando nimium mente perversa timet intellegere, ne cogatur quod intellexerit facere.* SRM 156, 1.

Perverted minds at times fear understanding too much, lest they be forced to put into practice what they understand.

REWARD AND PUNISHMENT

98. *Propter iniquitates tuas converso tibi indulgentiam Deus promisit: sed crastinum diem tibi nemo promisit.* SRM 87, 9, 11.

God has promised you his indulgence upon conversion from your iniquities: but no one has promised you tomorrow.

99. *Quis alius noster est finis, nisi pervenire ad regnum cuius nullus est finis?* COG 22, 30.

What else can the purpose of our life be, but to reach the kingdom without end?

100. *[Civitas] cuius rex veritas, cuius lex caritas, cuius modus aeternitas.* LET 138, 3.

[The city] whose king is the truth, whose law, charity, and whose measure, eternity.

101. *Ibi vacabimus et videbimus, videbimus et amabimus, amabimus et laudabimus.* COG 22, 35.

[In the heavenly city] we shall be at rest and contemplate, contemplate and love, love and praise.

102. *Ibi est locus quietis imperturbabilis, ubi non deseritur amor, si ipse non deseratur.* CFS 4, 11.

There is a place of unbroken peace, where a lover is not betrayed unless *he* is the one who betrays.

103. *Hic sitiendum est, alibi saginabimur.* OPS 62, 5.

Here on earth we must thirst; in heaven we shall be satisfied.

104. *Nonne vides quia perdidisti quod non dedisti?* OPS 36, 3.

Don't you see that you have lost what you didn't give?

105. *Domine Deus, pacem da nobis – omnia enim praestitisti nobis – pacem quietis, pacem sabbati, pacem sine vespere.* CFS 13, 35.

Lord God, who have entrusted all your works to us, give us the peace of rest, the peace of the Sabbath, the peace that never ends.

106. *Nunc autem quoniam quem tu imples, sublevas eum, quoniam tui plenus non sum, oneri mihi sum.* CFS 10, 28.

Right now I am a burden to myself because I am not filled with You, since you lighten the burden whenever you fill us with Yourself.

107. *Deus non deserit si non deseratur.* NAG 26, 29.

God does not abandon unless He is abandoned first.

108. *Cum punit Deus peccatores, non malum suum eis infert, sed malis eorum eos dimittit.* OPS 5, 10.

When God punishes sinners, He does not inflict on them evils of his own making; He abandons them to evils of their own making.

109. *Quocumque fugerit, se trahit post se; et quocumque talem traxerit se, cruciat se de se.* OPS 45, 3.

Wherever he flees to, he drags his own self with him; and wherever he drags it, he is tormented by that self.

110. *Quidquid enim vis potes fugere, homo,
praeter conscientiam tuam.* OPS 30, II, d. 1, 8.

O man, you can flee anything you wish,
except your own conscience.

111. *Inter omnes tribulationes humanae animae,
nulla est maior tribulatio quam conscientia
delictorum.* OPS 45, 3.

Of all the tribulations of the soul, none is
greater than the awareness of one's own
crimes.

112. *Iussisti enim et sic est: ut poena sua sibi sit
omnis inordinatus animus.* CFS 1, 12.

It is Your decree: every disorderly affec-
tion should be its own punishment.

113. *Omnis amor aut ascendit aut descendit.
Desiderium enim bono levamur ad Deum, et
desiderio malo ad ima praecipitamur.* OPS.
122, 1.

Every love either takes us up or brings us
down; If we want goodness, we climb up
to God; if evil, we fall headlong into the
abyss.

THE CHURCH

114. *[Christus] non est extra nos: in ipsius membri sumus, sub uno capite regimur, uno spiritu omnes vivimus, unam patriam omnes desideramus.* OPS 64, 7.

[Christ] is not a foreigner to us. We are His members, we are ruled by one head; we all live by one and the same spirit and we all long for the same homeland.

115. *Si amatis Deum, rapite omnes ad amorem Dei qui vobis iunguntur, et omnes qui sunt in domo vestra. Si amatur a vobis corpus Christi, id est unitas Ecclesiae, rapite eos ad fruendum.* OPS 33, d. 2, 6.

If you love God, drag your close friends, and those of your household, to love God too. If you love the Body of Christ, which is the unity of the Church, bring them in to enjoy its benefits too.

116. *Norunt fideles corpus Christi si corpus Christi esse non neglegunt.* TJEv 26, 13.

The faithful recognize the Body of Christ if they do not neglect being themselves the body of Christ.

117. *Locus eius tu eris si bonus, si confessus invocaveris eum.* OPS 74, 9.

You will be His dwelling place if you call upon Him after being cleansed in Confession.

118. *O sacramentum pietatis! O signum unitatis! O vinculum caritatis! Qui vult vivere, habet ubi vivat. Accedat, credat, incorporetur ut vivificetur.* TJEv 26, 13.

O sacrament of piety! O sign of unity! O bond of love! He who wants to live has a place and the means to live. Let him come close, believe, be united to Christ's body and so truly live.

119. *Tantum autem valet iunctura caritatis, ut quamvis multi lapides vivi in structura templi Dei convenient, unus lapis ex omnibus fiat.* OPS 39, 1.

So strongly does charity bind, that God's temple, though made up of many different stones, appears as a walled city.

120. *Superbia parit discissionem, caritas unitatem.* SRM 46, 18.

Pride breeds schism; charity gives rise to unity.

121. *Non autem facit discissionem nisi dissensio. Caritas autem compagem facit, compages complectitur unitatem, unitas servat caritatem, caritas pervenit ad claritatem.* OPS 30, II, d. 2, 1.

Dissent alone produces division. On the contrary, charity leads to agreement, agreement gives rise to unity; unity keeps charity alive and charity leads to glory.

122. *In quo enim nobiscum sentiunt, in eo etiam nobiscum sunt: in eo autem a nobis cessarunt in quo a nobis dissentiunt.* BPT 1, 1.

Where heretics agree with us, they are on our side; where they disagree with us, they are separated from us.

123. *Multi etiam qui aperte foris sunt, et haereti-ci appellantur, multis et bonis catholicis meliores sunt.* BPT 4, 3.

Many who are openly outside the Church, and are called heretics, are better people than many good Catholics.

124. *Nihil in Ecclesia catholica salubrius fieri, quam ut rationem praecedat auctoritas.* CCC 2, 16.

Nothing makes the Catholic Church stronger than acting by reason of authority.

125. *Inter persecutiones mundi et consolationes Dei peregrinando procurrit Ecclesia.* COG 18, 51.

The Church runs forward, buffeted between the persecutions of the world and the consolations of God.

126. *Ergo gratulemur et agamus gratias non solum nos christianos factos esse, sed Christ-um.* TJEv 21, 8.

Let's then rejoice and give thanks, for having been made not only Christians, but Christ Himself.

127. *Plenitudo ergo Christi caput et membra. Quid est "caput et membra?" Christus et Ecclesia.* TJEv 21, 8.

Fullness of Christ means head and members. What does "head and members" mean? Christ and the Church.

128. *Qui noluerit servire caritati, necesse est ut serviat iniquitati.* OPS 18, 2.

Who does not want to serve charity, must perforce serve evil instead.

129. *Nullo modo autem possunt dicere se habere caritatem qui dividunt unitatem.* TJEv 7, 3.

Those who break unity can in no way be said to live charity.

130. *In concordia Christi omnes una anima sumus.* OPS 62, 15.

In one heart with Christ we are all one soul.

131. *Et diligendo fit et ipse membrum, et fit per dilectionem in compage corporis Christi, et erit unus Christus amans se ipsum.* TJEp 10, 3.

By loving, one becomes a member; by that same love one shares in the unity of Christ's body, and thus there will be one Christ loving Himself.

132. *Qui ergo fecit te sine te non te iustificat sine te.* SRM 169, 11.

He who created you without you will not save you without you.

133. *Virtute maiora, utilitate meliora, actu faciliora, numero pauciora.* AGF 19, 13.

[The Sacraments] are most powerful, most useful, most practical, yet few in number.

134. *Qui accipit mysterium unitatis et non tenet vinculum pacis, non mysterium accipit pro se sed testimonium contra se.* SRM 272, 1.

Whoever receives the mystery of unity and does not keep the bond of peace, receives not a sacrament to his profit but a witness to his condemnation.

135. *Intellegat non se esse episcopum qui praeesse dilexerit, non prodesse.* COG 19, 19.

Let a bishop understand that to love power without being of service, is to be no bishop at all.

136. *Quae autem maior est virtus pietatis, quam caritas unitatis?* SRM 269, 3.

What act of piety is stronger than love for unity?

137. *Quia nec propter malos qui videntur esse intus, deserendi sunt boni, qui vere sunt intus.* ACS 2, 33.

The presence of evil people who appear to belong to the Church, is no reason to desert the good people who truly belong to it.

138. *Fugio paleam, ne hoc sim; non aream, ne nihil sim.* ACS 3, 35.

I run away from the chaff, so as to avoid being chaff; but not from the threshing floor, so as to avoid being nothing at all.

139. *Si quam operam vestram mater Ecclesia desideraverit, nec elatione avida suscipiatis nec blandiente desidia despuatis.* LET 48, 1.

When Mother Church asks some deed of you, neither accept out of greed for position, nor decline out of laziness and false humility.

140. *Extra Ecclesiam Catholicam totum potest praeter salutem. Potest habere honorem, potest habere Sacramenta, potest cantare Alleluia, potest respondere Amen, potest Evangelium tenere, potest in nomine Patris et Filii et Spiritus Sancti fidem habere et praedicare; sed nusquam nisi in Ecclesia Catholica salutem poterit invenire.* SRM 6.

Outside the Catholic Church everything can be found except salvation. One can find honor and the sacraments. One may sing Alleluia and reply: Amen. One may have the Gospel, have faith in the Father, Son and Holy Spirit. One may even preach this faith; but nowhere may one find salvation except in the Catholic Church.

141. *Beatior ergo Maria percipiendo fidem Christi quam concipiendo carnem Christi.* OHV, 3, 3.

Mary was happier for laying hold of Christ's faith than for conceiving His flesh.

142. *Sic et materna propinquitas nihil Mariae profuisset nisi felicius Christum corde quam carne gestasset.* OHV 3, 3.

Motherly closeness would have been of no use to Mary unless she had been happier to bear Christ in her heart than in her flesh.

143. *[Animalia aeria] decipere animas facillime consuerunt, aut periturarum fortunarum curiosas, aut fragilium cupidas potestatum, aut inanium formidolosas miraculorum.* DOR 2, IX, 27.

[The devils] have succeeded with the utmost ease in deceiving souls into seeking vain success, lusting after perishable power, or easily frightening them with spectacular wonders.

SCRIPTURE

144. *Sint castae deliciae meae Scripturae tuae; nec fallar in eis, nec fallam ex eis.* CFS 11, 2.

Let Your Scriptures be my pure delight. With them I can neither deceive nor be deceived.

145. *Mira profunditas eloquiorum tuorum . . . Horror est intendere in eam; horror honoris et tremor amoris.* CFS 12, 14.

One delves into Scripture with awe: it is the awe of being honored by God and the trembling of love.

146. *Sapienter autem dicit homo tanto magis vel minus, quanto in Scripturis sanctis magis minusve profecit.* OCD 4, 5.

It is wisely said that a man is more or less wise in direct proportion to his proficiency in Scripture.

147. *Quid valet caritas omnis Scriptura commendat.* TJEp 5, 13.

Every passage of Scripture tells us how much charity is worth.

148. *Omnia quae illis continentur libris vel de ipso [Christo] dicta sunt vel propter ipsum.* AGF 12, 7.

Everything in those books is either about Him [Christ] or for the sake of Him.

149. *Quisquis igitur Christo adhaeret, totum bonum quod etiam in litteris legis non intellegit, habet; quisquis est autem alienus a Christo, nec intellegit nec habet.* OPS 77, 7.

Those who are close to Christ possess all the good contained in Scripture, even what they don't understand. Away from Christ, they neither understand nor possess anything.

150. *Remansit adultera et Dominus, remansit vulnerata et medicus, remansit magna miseria et magna misericordia.* OPS 50, 8.

There remained the woman taken in adultery and the Lord, the wounded and the physician, great wretchedness and great mercy.

VIRTUES

151. *Intellectus enim merces est fidei. Ergo noli quaerere intellegere ut credas, sed crede ut intellegas.* TJEv 29, 6.

Understanding is the reward of faith. Therefore do not try to understand in order to believe, rather believe in order to understand.

152. *Si potes, cape; si non potes, crede.* TJEv 35, 5.

If you can understand, well and good; if you cannot, just believe.

153. *Fecisti nos ad te, et inquietum est cor nostrum donec requiescat in te.* CFS 1, 1.

You have made us for Yourself, and our heart is not at peace until it rests in You.

154. *Esto humilis, porta Dominum tuum; esto iumentum sessoris tui.* TJEp 7, 2.

Be humble, carry your Lord with you. Be a mount, for Him to sit astride you.

155. *Est enim quaedam pulchritudo iustitiae . . .*
Habet iustitia formam suam, oculos quaerit,
accendit amatores suos. OPS 32, II, d. 1, 6.

There is a certain beauty in justice . . . but
justice has a beauty all its own; it requires
contemplation, and sets on fire those who
love it.

156. *Quando iustum virum movebunt aut ulla*
onera, aut ulla pericula, aut ulla fastidia, aut
ulla blandimenta fortunae? DOR 2, XIX, 51.

How could the burdens, dangers, troubles
and allurements of fortune move a just
man?

157. *Sicut aures corporis ad os hominis, sic cor*
hominis ad aures Dei. OPS 119, 9.

As the human voice speaks to human ears,
so does the human heart speak to God's
ears.

158. *Non corporis voce, quae cum strepitu ver-*
berati aeris promitur, sed voce cordis, quae
hominibus silet, Deo autem sicut clamor
sonat. OPS 3, 4.

It is not noisy words issuing from the
mouth that cry out to God, but words

issuing from the heart. Men cannot hear them.

159. *Dic animae meae: salus tua ego sum. Sic dic, ut audiam. Ecce aures cordis mei ante te, Domine; aperi eas et dic animae meae: salus tua ego sum.* CFS 1, 5.

Say to my heart: I am your salvation. Speak that I may hear, Lord, with the ears of my heart right before you. Open them wide and say to my heart, I am your salvation.

160. *Doce ergo me suavitatem inspirando caritatem . . . Doce me disciplinam donando patientiam, doce me scientiam illuminando intelligentiam.* OPS 118, 17.

Teach me sweetness by filling me with charity . . . teach me discipline by granting me patience, teach me knowledge by enlightening my mind.

161. *Ex amante alio accenditur alius.* CFS 4, 14.

Lover and loved warm up to each other.

162. *Invocas Deum quando in te vocas Deum.* OPS 30, II, d. 3, 4.

You invoke God when you call on God inside you.

163. *In illo ergo amentur. Et rape ad eum tecum quos potes et dic eis: hunc amemus, hunc amemus.* CFS 4, 12.

Take along with you everyone you can and tell them, "Let us love Him, let us love Him."

164. *Vis invocare Deum? Gratis invoca. Avare, an parum est tibi, si te impleat ipse Deus?* OPS 30, II, d. 3, 4.

Do you want to call on God? Don't ask for anything when you do. Don't be greedy. Does it mean so little to you that God Himself should fill you completely?

165. *Ubi non ego, ibi felicius ego.* CNT 13, 19.

Where my selfishness is not present, then I am at my happiest.

166. *Et tota spes mea non nisi in magna valde misericordia tua. Da quod iubes, et iube quod vis.* CFS 10, 29.

All my hope is in nothing but in your

exceedingly great mercy. Grant me what
you command and command what you will.

167. *Hoc est Deum gratis amare, de Deo Deum
sperare.* SRM 334, 3.

    To expect only God from God is truly to
    love God selflessly.

168. *Beatus qui amat te, et amicum in te, et inimi-
cum propter te. Solus enim nullum carum
amittit cui omnes in illo cari sunt, qui non
amittitur.* CFS 4, 9.

    Blessed are those who love you, love their
    friends in you and their enemies for your
    sake. Such will never miss any of their
    dear ones, for all are dear in Him who is
    never missed.

169. *Quamdiu ergo nondum adhaesisti, ibi pone
spem.* OPS 72, 34.

    For as long as you are not perfectly unit-
    ed to Him, put all your hope in Him.

170. *Ipsum desiderium tuum oratio tua est; et si
continuum desiderium, continua oratio.* LET
130, 18.

Your prayer is your very desire; a continuous desire is a continuous prayer.

171. *Continuum desiderium tuum continua vox
tua est. Tacebis si amare destiteris.* OPS 37, 13.

Your ceaseless desire is your continuous
voice. You will fall silent when you cease
to love.

172. *Desiderium sinus cordis est; capiemus, si
desiderium quantum possumus extendamus.*
TJEv 40, 10.

Desire is the heart's inner recess; we shall
be capable of receiving God if we expand
our desire to its greatest extent.

173. *Desiderium semper orat, etsi lingua taceat. Si
semper desideras, semper oras. Quando dor-
mitat oratio? Quando friguerit desiderium.*
SRM 80, 7.

Desire prays without ceasing, though the
tongue be silent. If you desire unceasingly, you pray unceasingly. When does
prayer doze off? When desire cools down.

174. *Nam qui desiderat, etsi lingua taceat, cantat*

corde; qui autem non desiderat, quolibet clamore aures hominum feriat, mutus est Deo. OPS 86, 1.

The one who truly desires, sings with the heart though the tongue be silent; the one who does not desire, however much he may shout in human ears, is dumb before God.

175. *Quid enim desideres tu nosti; quid tibi prosit ille novit.* SRM 80, 1.

You know what you want. He knows what you need.

176. *Oratio tua locutio est ad Deum; quando legis, Deus tibi loquitur: quando oras, Deo loqueris.* OPS 85, 7.

To pray is to talk to God. When you read, God speaks to you; when you pray, you speak to God.

177. *Dilige et fac quod vis.* TJEp 7, 8.

Love and do whatever you wish.

178. *Diligendo proximum purgas oculum ad videndum Deum.* TJEv 17, 8.

By loving your neighbor you purify your gaze for seeing God.

179. *Cum esses languidus, portabat te proximus tuus; sanus factus es, porta proximum tuum.* TJEv 17, 8.

When you were ill, your neighbor carried you on his back. Now that you are well, carry your neighbor on yours.

180. *Ad Dominum enim nondum pervenimus, sed proximum nobiscum habemus. Porta ergo eum cum quo ambulas, ut ad eum pervenias cum quo manere desideras.* TJEv 17, 9.

We are not with the Lord yet, but we still have our neighbor with us. Help the one you walk with to bear his burden, so that you may attain Him with whom you desire to be.

181. *In eo quod amatur, aut non laboratur, aut et labor amatur.* OWD 21, 26.

In those things we enjoy, either there is no toil, or the very toil delights us.

182. *Non potest separari dilectio. Elige tibi quid diligas; sequuntur te cetera.* TJEp 10, 3.

Love cannot be divided. Choose what you should love, and everything else will follow.

183. *Pedes tui caritas tua est.* OPS 33, d. 2, 10.

Your feet take you to what you love.

184. *Sed si angustantur vasa carnis, dilatentur spatia caritatis.* SRM 69, 1.

If vessels of flesh shrink, let charity expand to fill the gap.

185. *Num vobis dicitur: Nihil ametis? Absit. Pigri, mortui, detestandi, miseri eritis, si nihil ametis. Amate, sed quid ametis videte.* OPS 31, II, 5.

Have you ever been told not to love? On the contrary. If you did not love, you would be lazy, dead, wretched, and miserable. Love, but beware of what you love.

186. *Adde ergo scientiae caritatem, et utilis erit scientia; non per se, sed per caritatem.* TJEv 27, 5.

Add charity to knowledge for it to be of use, and not in itself, but for charity's sake.

187. *Fecerunt itaque civitates duas amores duo: terrenam scilicet amor sui usque ad contemptum Dei, coelestem vero amor Dei usque ad contemptus sui.* COG 14, 28.

Two loves built two cities: the love of self built the earthly city to the contempt of God; and the love of God built the heavenly city to the contempt of self.

188. *Pondus meum amor meus, eo feror quocumque feror.* CFS 13, 9.

My love is my strength: it takes me everywhere.

189. *Talis est quisque qualis eius dilectio est. Terram diligis? Terra eris. Deum diligis? Quid dicam? Deus eris? Non audeo dicere ex me; Scripturas audiamus: "Ego dixi: dii estis et filii Altissimi omnes."* TJEp 2, 14.

One is what one loves. Do you love the earth? Then earth you are. Do you love God? I daren't answer on my own account, but refer you to Scripture: "*I declare: gods you are, offspring of the Most High all of you.*" [Ps. 82:6]

190. *Dicat si habet caritatem, et tunc dicat: natus sum ex Deo. Si autem non habet, characterem*

quidem impositum habet, sed desertor vagatur. TJEp 5, 6.

Let [the Christian] examine his charity, to be able to say: I am born of God. If he lacks it, he is a deserter running away, even if he bears the seal of a Christian.

191. *Unde enim praecepta servet non habet, qui non diligit.* TJEv 82, 3.

Whoever fails to love has no reason for keeping the commandments.

192. *Nescio quo enim inexplicabili modo, quisquis seipsum, non Deum amat, non se amat; et quisquis Deum, non seipsum amat, ipse se amat.* TJEv 123, 5.

I can't explain, but the one who loves himself and not God does not love himself, whereas the one who loves God but not himself, truly loves himself.

193. *Amat me Deus, amat te Deus.* OPS 34, d. 1, 12.

God loves me, and He loves you.

194. *Ama et propinquabit; ama et habitabit.* SRM 21, 2.

Love, and He will draw close; love and He will dwell in you.

195. *Caritas sine gaudio talis esse non potest.* OPS 76, 6.

A joyless charity is not charity at all.

196. *Minus te, Domine, amat qui tecum aliquid amat, quod non propter te amat.* CFS 10, 29.

Whoever loves something else besides you, Lord, loves you less, for he does not love you for your own sake.

197. *Quis enim sic delectat quam ille qui fecit omnia quae delectant?* OPS 32, II, d. 1, 6.

Who can give us more delight than He who made all that is delightful?

198. *Dilectio ergo sola discernit inter filios Dei et filios diaboli.* TJEp 5, 7.

Love alone can tell apart God's children from the devil's.

199. *Magna est enim miseria superbus homo, sed maior misericordia humilis Deus.* CAT 4, 8.

The wretchedness of a proud man is great, but the mercy of a humble God is greater.

200. *Remota itaque iustitia quid sunt regna nisi magna latrocinia?* COG 4, 4.

Take away justice, and what are governments but dens of robbers?

INDEX

(Numbers listed refer to listing, not page, number.)